RED TAIL BOA

Everything You Need To Know
About Red Tail Boa, Care,
Housing, Caging And Health Care

Dr. Philip Bryan

Table of Contents

CHAPTER ONE

WHAT IS RED TAIL BOA?

The red followed boa, likewise alluded to as a boa constrictor, is an exceptionally normal decision as a pet snake. Red followed boas can be effectively procured from a reproducer, pet store, or reptile appear and are recognizable by their red designed shading on the finish of their tail.Red tail boas are local to Brazil and close by regions where they invest their energy in downpour woodlands and swamps and keeping in mind that their surroundings fluctuate they are considered respectably arboreal.

TEMPERANCE AND CONDUCT OF RED TAIL BOA

The red tail boa develops to be 8 to 10 feet long and can weigh around 50 pounds when it is full-developed. They will live 25 to 30 years in imprisonment if very much thought about and are large snakes for the normal pet proprietor. Red followed boas should be truly considered before being bought because of their quality, size, the sum they eat, and their capacity to choke. They are not legitimate to claim all over so make certain to check your neighborhood laws also.

The explanation red tail boas are so well known is expected to some degree to their commonly compliant demeanor. They aren't generally forceful snakes yet regardless of whether they aren't vexed they can harm an individual effectively by choking (to hold tight to somebody's hand, neck, or arm) or gnawing you on the off chance that they think your hand is food.

CHAPTER TWO

LODGING RED TAIL BOA

A 10-foot snake needs a little space to move about however they don't ordinarily like extending to their full length. Snakes have a sense of safety when they are stowing away under something and can twist up. On the off chance that they are completely uncoiled, it's typically a sign they feel defenseless and compromised. A fenced in area that gives 8 to 10 feet of floor space, is a few feet high and two or three feet wide is bounty enormous for a grown-up red followed boa.

Maybe the most significant thing about a walled in area for a red followed boa is the manner by which secure it should be. All snakes are slick people will push through opened covers and just barely get through little openings. All snake fenced in areas ought to have bolts or hooks to forestall a getaway, which can be risky to both the snake and the individuals living in the house. Putting a red followed boa inside a tied pillowcase functions admirably for shipping or to briefly hold them while cleaning their walled in area. Fundamental lodging prerequisites include:

• Appropriately measured and molded environment for a grown-up red-followed boa to oblige ordinary conduct and exercise.

• Aspen shavings, mulch-type, for example, coconut fiber bedding or reptile bark; hosed sphagnum greenery.

• Provide a concealing territory sufficiently enormous for your snake to fit inside and a branch or stylistic layout to get on.

Keep up 40-60 percent moistness; higher during shedding.

• Temperature angle (95 degrees for the warm end and 78 degrees for the cool end); suggest brilliant warmth.

• Provide 8-12 hours of light every day. Try not to leave white light on consistently; a nighttime or infrared light ought to be utilized around evening time.

Since red tail boas originate from a tropical situation, the simplicity of keeping up moistness levels ought to be thought about when setting up an enclosure. Glass or plexiglass sides and tops assistance to keep moistness higher in a fenced in area yet you will need to ensure enough air is as yet ready to circle inside and that nothing will soften from the warming gadgets.Your snake needs a huge, tough bowl for water. It ought to have the option to handily accommodate its whole body in the bowl to splash. Red followed boas ought to likewise have a shroud box or spot to get away from the warmth and to twist up in a peaceful, concealed spot at whatever point they need to.

Numerous proprietors utilize wooden or cardboard boxes for stows away and supplant or clean them varying. Tree limbs could possibly be utilized by your snake. The sort of sheet material you pick ought to be anything but difficult to clean since a huge snake creates a significant enormous measure of waste material. Paper towels are incredible for youthful red tail boas and reptile confine cover or indoor/open air cover cut into removable segments are anything but difficult to clean when you have a grown-up snake. Different materials that are regularly utilized incorporate reptile bark, reptile soil blends, and other characteristic floor covers. Sand isn't suitable for red followed boas; they may ingest it causing a stomach related impaction.

CHAPTER THREE

HEAT AND LIGHTNING

Since red followed boas are from Brazil they like their surroundings warm. A lolling spot of 90 to 95 degrees ought to be kept up utilizing heat lights or different methods. However, abstain from utilizing hot rocks since they can cause warm consumes in a snake. The remainder of the tank can be in the upper 80 degrees and around evening time it's protected if the temperature drops into the lower 80's. Warmth lights, fired warmth producers, undertank radiators, and hatchery confines are generally adequate methods for warming a snake confine. Simply ensure your snake can't get to the warming component and consume itself. UVB lighting isn't required for red tail boas, yet in the event that you need to offer supplemental white light during the day, an UVB light is an extraordinary choice. It might even assistance invigorate craving, decline pressure and make your snake a general more joyful, increasingly dynamic snake.

FOOD AND WATER

Adolescent red tail boas will eat fuzzies, at that point mice, at that point rodents, and once they arrive at adulthood, they will eat bunnies and huge rodents. Prey things ought to be murdered preceding taking care of them to your snake and offered in a walled in area utilized uniquely for taking care of. Try not to take care of your snake in its normal enclosure; this will diminish the probability of the snake thinking you are food and incidentally gnawing you or ingesting its substrate. The taking care of tank ought to be secured with a towel while taking care of to give a suspicion that all is well and good to your snake, or you can put your snake's shroud confine the taking care of tank while taking care of

CHAPTER FOUR

HEALTH PROBLEMS

The most genuine infection that can influence boa constrictors is incorporation body illness or IBD. This is a deadly retrovirus, much the same as HIV in people. This infection can lay lethargic for a considerable length of time before the snake gives any indication of sickness. This sickness can be transmitted from snake to wind through bugs, which convey tainted natural liquids. This is the reason it's a smart thought to keep numerous pet snakes isolated if conceivable.

IBD is set apart by poor craving and extreme salivation, and in genuine or further developed cases, IBD makes snakes lose control of their substantial developments.Red followed boas likewise are defenseless to respiratory contaminations, set apart by wheezing and nasal release. A frothy release from a snakc's mouth ordinarily shows pneumonia, which requires prompt treatment.

Scale decay and rankle malady are both regular in boa constrictors, with both normally brought about by unsanitary conditions. Rankle illness may seem like consumes on the snake's skin and is generally brought about by overheated enclosures or an absence of moistness.These sicknesses ought to get treatment from a veterinarian who represents considerable authority in reptiles.

CHOOSING A RED TAILED BOA

Red followed boas are huge, solid, extensive snakes and aren't for everybody. Taking care of them can turn out to be increasingly costly as they get bigger, thus will the time it takes to clean their confine. In this manner, ensure you are arranged and recognize what's in store before bringing home any pet, particularly one that satisfies 30 years.

CHAPTER FIVE

BEHAVIOR AND TEMPERAMENT OF BOA

Boas are commonly dynamic, ready snakes. They may murmur or chomp on the off chance that they feel undermined, yet predictable taking care of as a rule will make them tame and not all that cautious. It's imperative to realize how to hold a boa, so it has a sense of safety. One hand ought to be under its body close to its head, and the other hand ought to be under the back portion of its body. The boa may freely fold itself over you for included help, yet it normally won't choke except if it has an inclination that it's falling.

While infant boa constrictors can be housed in glass aquariums, bigger snakes will require a custom fenced in area that is either economically bought or built at home. Boa constrictors are extremely ground-breaking and will get away whenever given the opportunity, so walled in areas must be secure. A decent nook size for a grown-up boa constrictor is around 6 to 8 feet in length, 2 to 3 feet wide, and 2 to 3 feet tall. The base size is around 10 square feet of floor space for a solitary snake.

Stow away boxes are basic to cause your snake to feel secure. At least two covers up ought to be given in the nook, one at each finish of the temperature inclination. Stows away can be half logs, business reptile caverns, topsy turvy plastic compartments with an opening cut in the side, or even cardboard boxes. Ensure they are very little bigger than the snake, as a nearby fit will enable the snake to have a sense of security. They ought to be cleaned or supplanted when they become dirtied.

A cleaned and sanitized tree limb that is sufficiently substantial to help the snake's weight ought to likewise be given in the walled in area. Absorb it a sanitizer arrangement, wash it well indeed, and dry it completely before including it in the event that you got it from outside. Locally acquired driftwood can likewise be utilized.

WARMTH

Boa constrictors originate from tropical atmospheres, so warm temperatures in their walled in areas are basic. During the day, a temperature inclination between 82 to 90 degrees Fahrenheit (28 to 32 degrees Celsius) ought to be kept up. Additionally, a lounging spot of 90 to 95 degrees Fahrenheit (32 to 35 degrees Celsius) ought to be given. Around evening time, temperatures can drop to 78 to 85 degrees Fahrenheit (26 to 30 degrees Celsius).

The temperatures in your snake's pen are basic, so exact thermometers with estimations in a few areas of the nook (the warm end, cool end, and relaxing spot) are an unquestionable requirement. A blend of radiant bulbs, clay warming components, and warming cushions can be utilized to keep up the temperatures. Any bulbs or warming components in the fenced in area must be protected to forestall consumes, to which snakes are very vulnerable. Hot rocks ought to never be utilized.

LIGHT

Boas by and large needn't bother with any exceptional UV lighting.

Their eating routine ought to furnish them with the nutrient D that they would create from the sun's UV beams in nature.

MOISTNESS

Keep up a stickiness level in the fenced in area of around 60% to 75%.

THE END